# Here and There Loving You Always

A book about an open adoption from a birthmother to her child

## BEVERLY REYNOLDS

HIGGINS PUBLISHING
DALLAS * TX

Thank you so much for your purchase!

If you enjoy this book,
please post a review on the site
where you purchased this book.

AMAZON
SCAN TO REVIEW

Here and There, Loving You Always: A book about an open adoption from a birthmother to her child
Published by Higgins Publishing 2017 - Written and Illustrated by Beverly Reynolds
Copyright © 2016-2022  * All Rights Reserved.

No part of this publication may be reproduced, stored in a retrieval system, or transmitted by any means, electronic, mechanical, photocopy, recording, or otherwise, without the publisher's prior permission except as provided by USA copyright law. The opinions expressed by the author are not necessarily those of Higgins Publishing.

___

Published by Higgins Publishing
higginspublishing.com

Higgins Publishing is committed to excellence in the publishing industry. The company reflects the philosophy established by the founder, based on Psalm 68:11, "The Lord gave the word and great was the company of those who published it."

The Higgins Publishing Speakers Bureau provides various authors for speaking events. To schedule an author for an event, go to higginspublishing.com.

___

Library of Congress Control Number 2017935908
Reynolds, Beverly
  pages cm. 54
978-1-941580-67-7 (HC)

Here and There, Loving You Always: A book about an open adoption from a birthmother to her child
Higgins Publishing Hardcover Edition – May 2017 * November 2022 (1st Revised Edition)

1. Juvenile Non-Fiction: Family / Adoption
2. Juvenile Non-Fiction: Family / Orphans / Foster Homes
3. Juvenile Non-Fiction: Social Topics / Emotions & Feelings

For information about special discounts for fundraising, bulk purchases, subsidiary, foreign and translations rights & permissions, please contact, Higgins Publishing at contact@higginspublishing.com.

Published in the United States of America

## THIS BOOK IS DEDICATED TO...

The love all birthmothers have for their children.
To my handsome son – may you always know the people that truly are...
**Here and There, Loving You Always.**

## A SPECIAL THANK YOU TO...

My son's birthmother who inspired me
to teach our child to work hard towards his goals.

My parents, Julianne and Keith Boerner,
and my family and friends for showing me how to be a better parent.

My boyfriend, Don Horner,
for putting up with me during the writing and illustration process.

Donna Kowalski for editing the text prior to submitting to my publisher.

You grew inside me
and you were the one.
I had dreams that you would
skip, play and run.

You tickled inside me
each day and night.
I grew to love you
each part of my might.

Waiting so patiently
just to hold you.
Wrapped up tightly
in a soft blanket too.

I wanted to keep you
for my own.
After all,
you are my flesh and bone.

I knew I could not raise you
Here or There
So I picked a mommy and
daddy to care.

They promised to love you
Here in the park.
I know they will love you
and never part.

They will challenge you
in an archery game.
They will be there for you
and call you by name.

14

Mommy and Daddy
will Love You Always,
To watch as you grow bigger
in each of your days.

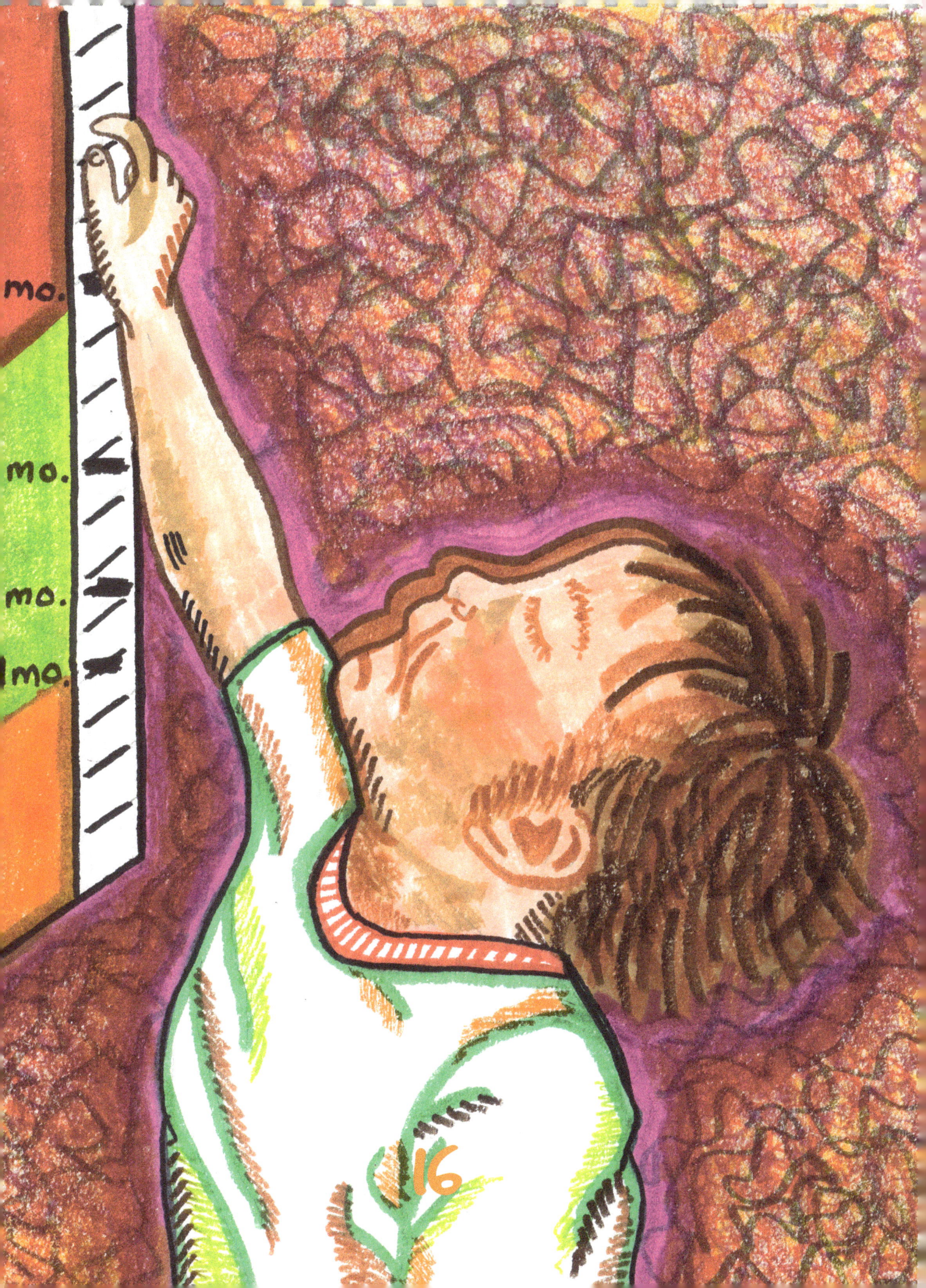

Your parents and I waited
for you to arrive.
Quickly that day came
and each of us cried.

From newborn to crawling
oh so fast.
Then talking as if each day
were the last.

When you learned your letters,
they came with ease.
Even your numbers
seemed to be a breeze.

It is good to see you
write, paint and draw.
The smartest child
that I ever saw.

Mommy is there
and bandages your knee.
She calms your fears
as sweet as can be.

Daddy takes you fishing
around the block.
He taught you to catch
a fish from the dock.

Every day I think of you
Here and There
Please know
I remember you in prayer.

30

When you got your puppy
I loved her too.
Seeing her cheered me
each time I felt blue.

Pictures of you
make me proud each day...
from your first breath
to the lead part in a play.

Whether soccer or baseball,
you are the best.
I especially love your
science fair mess.

36

You seem to enjoy
your time in the sun.
I am glad you still like
to skip, play and run.

Even in fall when all
the leaves come down,
I will cherish you
from sun up until dawn.

Watching to see
how you are inspired.
Music is quite simply how
you are wired.

Our hearts are connected
and to remain.
A perfect child from
Here and There to stay.

I keep a picture
of you by my heart,
Loving You Always
we will not be apart.

Even when you make
an artistic creation,
or go on a really
nice vacation...

Through every 'swing,'
life throws your way,
Here and There,
Loving You Always!

www.ingramcontent.com/pod-product-compliance
Lightning Source LLC
Chambersburg PA
CBHW041224240426
43661CB00012B/1135